Flapping and fluttering,
the little Arctic tern
takes off!

Greenland

NORTH
AMERICA

Off on her epic migration,
a daring journey chasing
sun and food

SOUTH
AMERICA

N

EUROPE

ASIA

AFRICA

from North Pole to South Pole,
across four oceans
and three continents,
and back in a year—
sixty-thousand miles—
the longest migration
of any living creature on Earth.

AUSTRALIA

ANTARCTICA

The Longest Journey

An Arctic Tern's Migration

Amy Hevron

NEAL PORTER BOOKS

HOLIDAY HOUSE / NEW YORK

Solstice, June 20

Her story began when our little bird
hatched on the Greenland tundra
in summer, a time when the sun never sets.

Her first days were spent
in a noisy colony of thousands,
growing up fast, preparing
for her first voyage,
only two months away,

ARCTIC CIRCLE

North Pole

Greenland

cared for by her parents,
surviving flooding rains
and Arctic predators,
often with a hungry belly.

Greenland, August '18

Kip-kip-kip! she calls,
embarking on her journey
to the other end of the planet.

Our young traveler now ventures south,
one of a flock of twenty
climbing up, up, up . . .
gliding on currents of wind,
soaring faster and faster!

Soaring farther too,
as stars guide the way ahead.

She flaps hard to keep up.
Kree-ah, kree-ah! her father calls,
leading the flock to a bustling
feeding area out at sea . . .

where they stay for a month
to fill their bellies for the long trek ahead,
catching cold-water krill and fish
that are schooling deeper in the ever-changing,
ever-warming North Atlantic Ocean.

She hovers then plunge-dives underwater,
missing again and again.
Starving, straining, until at last . . .

she catches a bite.
Gulp!

North Atlantic, August 22

After weeks of honing her fishing skills,
she departs,
floating up, up, up through the clouds,
studying landmarks
that dot the world below.

Azores,
September 15

Resting on Tenerife in the Canary Islands
for the night, discovering its crowded, sandy shores . . .

Autumn Equinox,
September 22

Tenerife

Tropic of Cancer

then, navigating south
along the desert cliffs
of northwest Africa,
past Morocco
and Mauritania,

swooping near wavetops,
snatching up
mackerel in flight,

then suddenly—

Pyeh! Pyeh!
A scavenging pirate!
A great skua lunges
toward her, trying to make
her drop her food.

Her protective father
dive-bombs down.
Kek-kek-kek! Keee-err! Keee-err!
he shrieks,
fending off the attack.

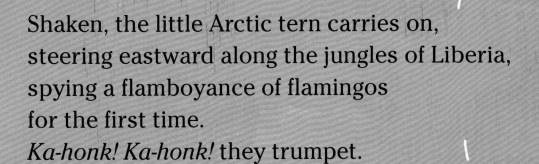

Shaken, the little Arctic tern carries on,
steering eastward along the jungles of Liberia,
spying a flamboyance of flamingos
for the first time.
Ka-honk! Ka-honk! they trumpet.

Liberia

Equator

Pressing on past the equator,
she meets a pod of humpback whales
that churn up a sand-eel feast.

She's careful not to be swallowed up too.

Days pass by.
Now fifteen thousand miles from home . . .
she flails against headwinds near the
dunes of Namibia,

then rests on driftwood
near the rocky
Cape of Good Hope.

She battles to keep ahead
of an angry storm
over the ever-warming
South Atlantic Ocean,

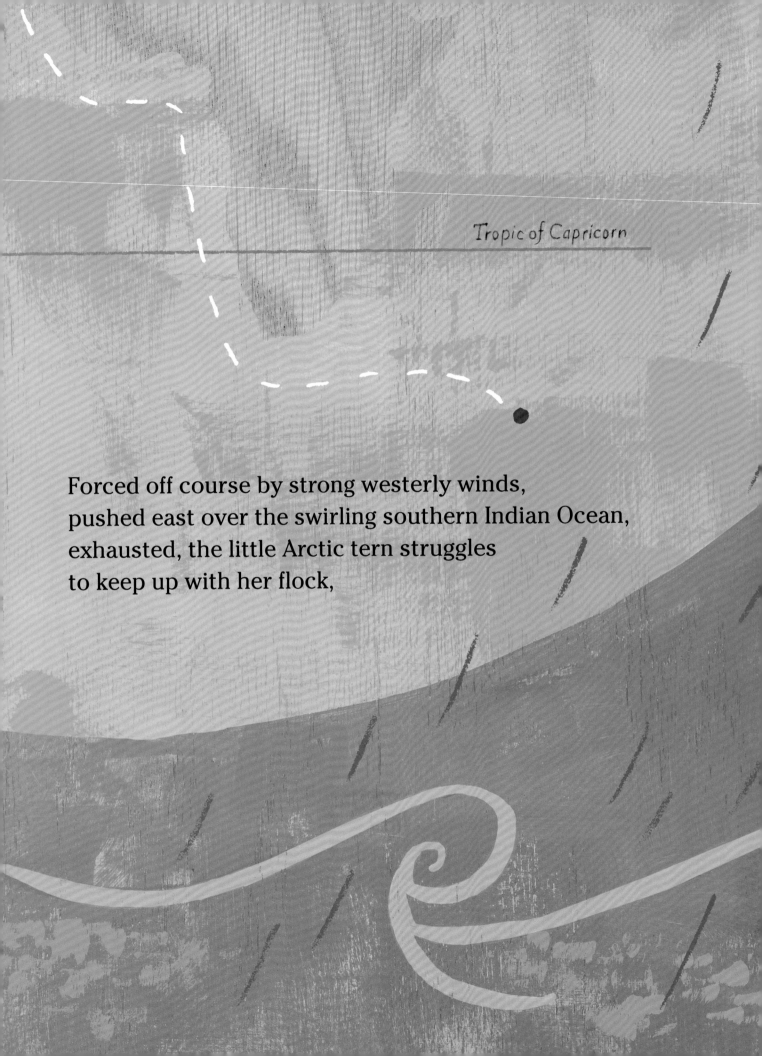

Tropic of Capricorn

Forced off course by strong westerly winds,
pushed east over the swirling southern Indian Ocean,
exhausted, the little Arctic tern struggles
to keep up with her flock,

while below—

Tuk-tuk-tuk! Trilll! Tuk-tuk-tuk!
A raft of macaroni penguins
leads them to refuge
on the archipelago of the Crozet Islands.

She gobbles up Antarctic krill,
regains her strength . . .

then pushes even farther south
and westward over the polar Southern Ocean
along the ice shelf of Antarctica, until at last . . .

she arrives at the Weddell Sea,
her final stop after thirty
thousand miles of flying.

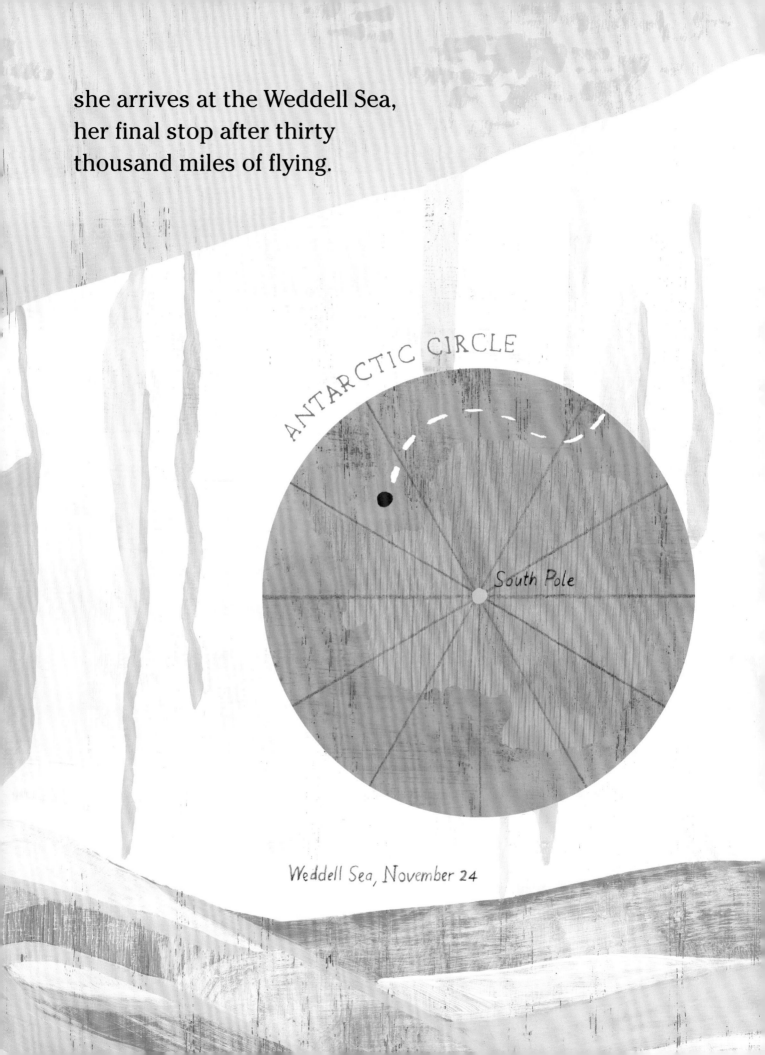

ANTARCTIC CIRCLE

South Pole

Weddell Sea, November 24

She rests on pack ice,
recuperating and molting
in the Antarctic summer,
also a place and a time
where the sun never sets.

And when days grow shorter and colder,
she takes off again with a new flock of twenty . . .

Autumn Equinox,
March 20

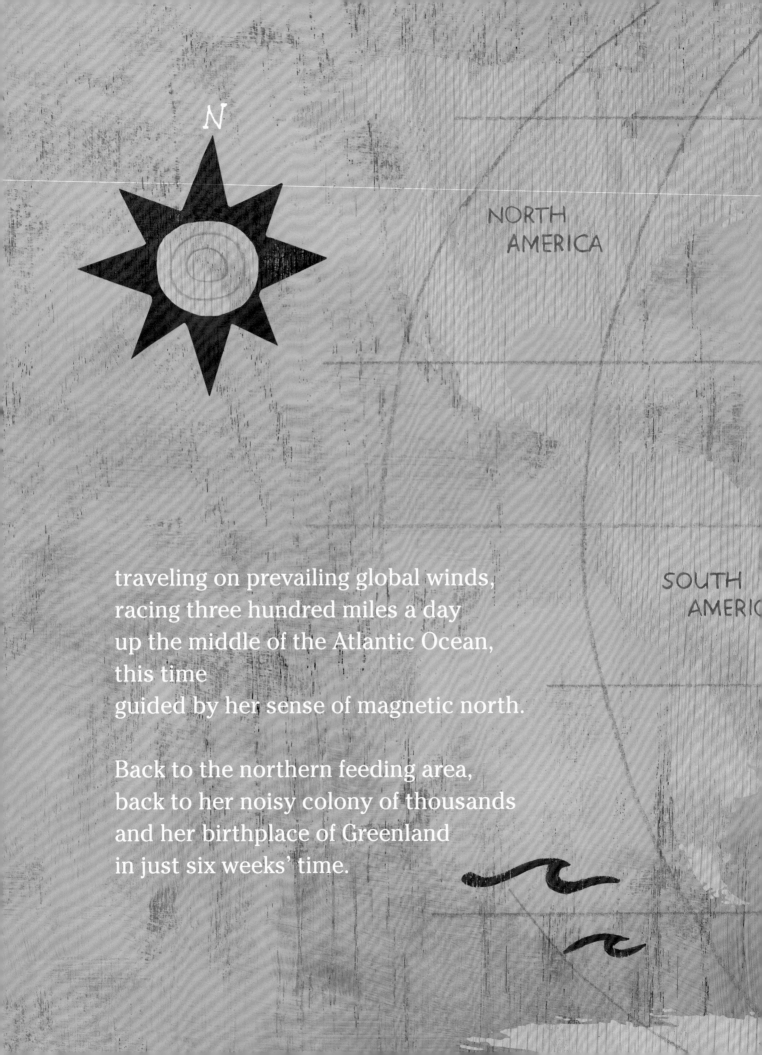

traveling on prevailing global winds,
racing three hundred miles a day
up the middle of the Atlantic Ocean,
this time
guided by her sense of magnetic north.

Back to the northern feeding area,
back to her noisy colony of thousands
and her birthplace of Greenland
in just six weeks' time.

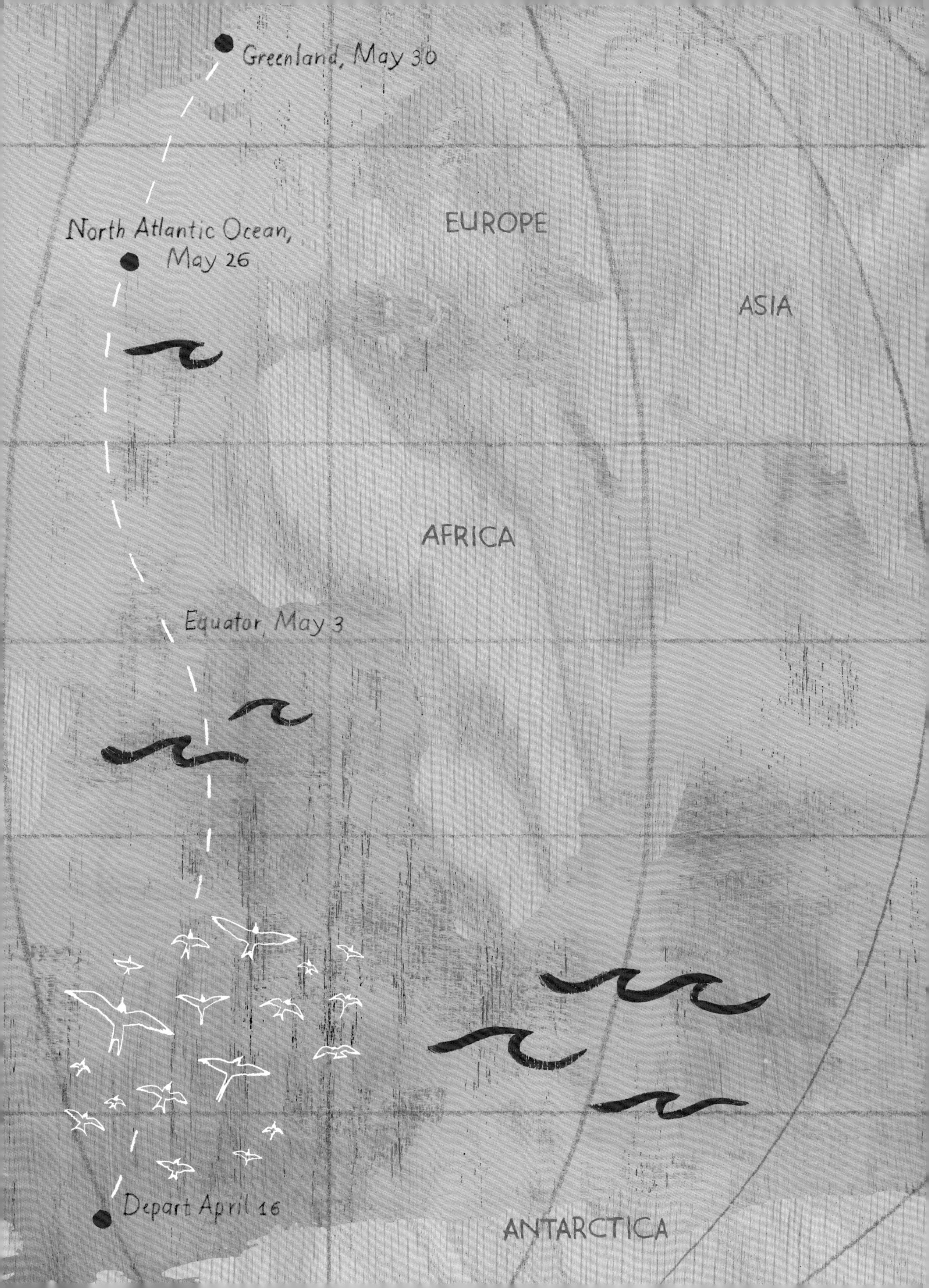

Greenland, May 30

North Atlantic Ocean,
May 26

EUROPE

ASIA

AFRICA

Equator May 3

Depart April 16

ANTARCTICA

The little seabird's
sixty-thousand-mile journey
across the earth is complete.

She will make it every
year of her life,
chasing sun and food
for thirty years,
traveling enough miles
in her lifetime to fly
to the moon and back
three times.

Resting, slowly unruffling
her well-traveled wings,
the little Arctic tern
takes in the sun.
Kip-kip-kip! she calls,
and waits for the journey
to begin again—

thirty thousand miles to go
in just three months.

More About Arctic Terns

Arctic terns live much of their life in the sky over open ocean. With lightweight bodies, aerodynamic tail feathers, and a wide wingspan, they are adapted for living in the air rather than on land.

In recent years, researchers have been tracking Arctic terns and have discovered that these small seabirds can fly more than 59,000 miles in a year, which is like flying around the Earth two and a half times. This book depicts one migration route. Other routes can be seen in the map below.

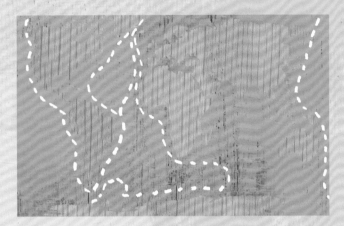

Arctic terns live to the age of thirty or more. Therefore, they can fly the equivalent of three times to the Moon and back in their lifetime.

Arctic terns see two summers a year, spending breeding season in the boreal summer of the Arctic and "wintering" in the austral summer of Antarctica. They breed on remote islands and coastal tundras in the northernmost regions of North America, Europe, and Asia. They nest on the ground, sometimes in mixed colonies with other terns, like common terns, in order to help defend their nests. Tern parents are highly protective of their young and use aggressive techniques like dive-bombing to deter predators, including Arctic foxes, polar bears and mink.

Breeding adult

Life stages

Egg - Egg is incubated by both parents for 20 to 24 days.

Chick - Chick leaves the nest at 1 to 3 days old and finds a hiding place nearby. Parents bring food back to their young.

Egg

Chick

Fledgling - Fledgling makes first flight at 21 to 28 days old.

Fledgling

Juvenile

Juvenile - Makes first flight south at 2 to 3 months old. After flying south for the first time, most juveniles stay in the southern hemisphere for a year, before returning north to their Arctic birthplace.

Breeding Adult - Females and males look the same. They are 12 inches long from bill tip to tail tip and have a 31-inch wingspan. They weigh around 4 ounces and are similar in size to a common grackle.

Arctic Terns use seasonal clues, like the sun's position in the sky, to know when to migrate. And hormonal changes in their bodies trigger the rapid molting of new feathers and a voracious appetite to bulk up for the long journey ahead. And while different Arctic tern colonies migrate different routes over the Atlantic and Pacific Oceans, they all use meandering routes.

Food

Arctic terns eat fish, crustaceans, and insects. These high-energy foods digest quickly and heat their bodies to help them survive the long journey and polar temperatures. During their journey, terns sometimes spend weeks or months at one feeding site over open ocean to stock up on food.

Mackerel

Mayfly

Krill

Sand eel

Plunge-diving

Arctic terns use a technique called plunge-diving in which they hover then dive headfirst into water to catch prey. They also skim the ocean's surface for food and chase insects in the air. And, if they encounter a pod of humpback whales feeding, they will take advantage of the churned-up krill and sand eels at the ocean's surface.

Arctic terns are fairly shallow divers, plunging up to a meter or so for their food. Thus, the biggest threat facing these seabirds is warming ocean temperatures. As the ocean surface temperature is rising, their main food sources of krill, herring, and sand eels are moving deeper down in the ocean to cooler temperatures, out of the Arctic terns' reach. Warming ocean temperatures are also leading to more severe storms. These storms in spring bring torrential floods that wipe out egg and chick populations. And on the journey, severe storms can prevent terns from accessing fish in churned-up oceans.

Where to See Arctic Terns

The best chance to see Arctic terns in the United States is from May to July in the coastal areas of Maine and Alaska. Outside of the U.S., they can be seen in northern Canada and northern Europe. You can visit the Maine Coastal Islands National Wildlife Refuge Visitor Center in Rockland, Maine, to learn more about Arctic tern research and preservation in the United States.

Further Reading

Bailey, Jill and D. Burnie. *Birds: Explore Nature with Fun Facts and Activities*, DK Publishing, 2017.

Callery, Sean. *Polar Lands*. Kingfisher Press, 2018.

Lerner, Carol. *On the Wing: American Birds in Migration*. HarperCollins, 2001.

Unwin, Mike and J. Desmond. *Migration: Incredible Animal Journeys*. Bloomsbury Children's Books, 2019.

www.allaboutbirds.org/

www.audubon.org/

www.activewild.com/arctic-animals-list/

Selected Bibliography

Record-breaking Bird Migration Revealed in New Research. New Castle University, BBC Springwatch, 2016. www.ncl.ac.uk/press/articles/archive/2016/06/arcticterns/

Egevang, C., I. Stenhouse, et al. "Tracking of Arctic Terns *Sterna paradisaea* Reveals Longest Animal Migration." Proceedings of the National Academy of Sciences, 2010.

Hatch, J. J. "Arctic Tern (Sterna paradisaea)," current version In *The Birds of North America*, ed. A. F. Poole and F. B. Gill. Cornell Lab of Ornithology, Ithaca, NY, 2002. doi.org/10.2173/bna.707

Kaufman, Kenn. *Kaufman Field Guide to Birds of North American*. Houghton Mifflin, 2000.

Ramroop, T. and K. West. "To the Ends of the Earth." National Geographic Society, 2011. www.nationalgeographic.org/news/ends-earth/

Sibley, D. A. *The Sibley Guide to Birds*. Knopf, 2014.

Welch, Linda and Stephen Kress. "Research Reveals Incredible Migratory Journey of Arctic Terns." National Audubon Society, 2012. projectpuffin.audubon.org/news/research-reveals-incredible-migratory-journey-arctic-terns

To Scott

Acknowledgements

A special thanks to Linda Welch, wildlife biologist at the U.S. Fish and Wildlife Service, and the team at the Maine Coastal Islands National Wildlife Refuge for their expertise and guidance in this project.

Neal Porter Books

Text and illustrations copyright © 2022 by Amy Hevron

All Rights Reserved
HOLIDAY HOUSE is registered in the U.S. Patent and Trademark Office.
Printed and bound in March 2022 at C&C Offset, Shenzhen, China.
The artwork for this book was made with acrylic and pencil on wood and digitally collaged.
Book design by Jennifer Browne
www.holidayhouse.com
First Edition
10 9 8 7 6 5 4 3 2 1

Library of Congress Cataloging-in-Publication Data

Names: Hevron, Amy, author, illustrator.
Title: The longest journey : an Arctic tern's migration / by Amy Hevron.
Description: First edition. | New York : Holiday House, [2022] | A Neal
  Porter book. | Includes bibliographical references. | Audience: Ages 5
  to 8 | Audience: Grades K–1 | Summary: "The story of an arctic tern's
  first migration to the South Pole and back again"— Provided by
  publisher.
Identifiers: LCCN 2021038050 | ISBN 9780823447008 (hardcover)
Subjects: LCSH: Arctic tern—Migration—Juvenile literature. | Arctic
  tern—Migration—Anecdotes.
Classification: LCC QL696.C46 H48 2022 | DDC 598.3/381568—dc23
LC record available at https://lccn.loc.gov/2021038050

ISBN 978-0-8234-4700-8 (hardcover)